salmonpoetry

Publishing Irish & International

Poetry Since 1981

Milking the Sun
Ag Crú na Gréine

With paintings by
BRENDA FITZMAURICE

The Irish of
SEÁN Ó RÍORDÁIN

Translated by
GABRIEL FITZMAURICE

Published in 2018 by
Salmon Poetry
Cliffs of Moher, County Clare, Ireland
Website: www.salmonpoetry.com
Email: info@salmonpoetry.com

Salmon Poetry and Gabriel Fitzmaurice are grateful to publisher Mícheál Ó Conghaile
and Cló Iar-Chonnacht for permission to publish Seán Ó Ríordáin's Irish originals
(from *Seán Ó Ríordáin: Na Dánta*, Cló Iar-Chonnacht, 2011)

ISBN 978-1-912561-34-6

COVER & INTERNAL ILLUSTRATIONS: Brenda Fitzmaurice
AUTHOR PHOTOGRAPH: *Tom Moore*
COVER DESIGN & TYPESETTING: *Siobhán Hutson*

Printed in Ireland by Sprint Print

Salmon Poetry gratefully acknowledges the support of
The Arts Council / An Chomhairle Ealaíon

Dom sheana-chara
Mícheál de Mórdha
agus Angela, a bhean uasal,
le grá

Acknowledgements

I wish to express my deepest thanks to Mícheál Ó Conghaile and Cló Iar-Chonnacht for permission to publish the Irish originals (from *Seán Ó Ríordáin: Na Dánta*, Cló Iar-Chonnacht 2011) and my translations, some of which were originally published in *The Flowering Tree/An Crann Faoi Bhláth* (Wolfhound Press, Dublin 1991), *Poems I Wish I'd Written* (Cló Iar-Chonnacht 1996), *A Wrenboy's Carnival* (Wolfhound Press, Dublin, Peterloo Poets, Cornwall 2000), *Poems from the Irish* (Marino Books, Cork 2004). *The Essential Gabriel Fitzmaurice* (Mercier Press, Cork 2008), *Poems of Faith and Doubt* (Salmon Poetry 2011) and *Best Loved Poems* (Currach Press, Dublin 2016)

Seán Ó Ríordáin: Selected Poems edited by Frank Sewell was published in 2014 by Yale University Press and Cló Iar-Chonnacht.

Contents

Foreword

These translations are excellent. Fitzmaurice captures the free swing of Ó Ríordáin's cadences ("Syllable-ing" being a fine example). They also seem to liberate something in Fitzmaurice's own muse – a blend of intensity, rueful lyricism and playfulness. (That postmodern, ludic element, always there in Ó Ríordáin, has never been so fully brought out before).

Renato Poggioli once wrote that that the translator is "a character in search of an author: in liberating the writer without, he also liberates the author within". That is exactly what these versions do. It's the old case of – give a man a mask and he'll tell you the truth.

Fitzmaurice's favourite Ó Ríordáin poems are the same (exactly) as mine. I think most readers will concur. The longer 'sequence' poems are the hardest to do (i.e. to maintain tone and at the same time capture the gear changes) – Fitzmaurice has done that well too.

I always liked Fitzmaurice's translations – but these ones have an extra "fifth dimension" – as if both poets together are more than the sum of their parts.

Another good thing – it seems much easier to read translations when they are all together in a volume, as here. This is a volume I could imagine anyone reading right through (and then dipping back for subsequent encounters).

DECLAN KIBERD

A Note on the Translations

Seán Ó Ríordáin (1916-1977) is one of the finest Irish poets of the twentieth century. Together with Máirtín Ó Direáin (1910-1988) and Máire Mhac an tSaoi (b. 1922) he was among the foremost poets of *Nuafhilíocht na Gaeilge*, the new Irish language poetry that emerged in the mid twentieth century. His first book, *Eireaball Spideoige*, appeared in 1952, the year I was born. In all, three collections of his own poetry were published in his lifetime. A posthumous volume, *Tar Éis Mo Bháis*, appeared in 1978.

I first came across *Nuafhilíocht na Gaeilge* as a student in Saint Michael's College, Listowel, Co. Kerry, in the 1960s. In English we were studying dead white males, but in Irish we were at the cutting edge of poetry in Ireland. I fell in love with Seán Ó Ríordáin. He spoke to me in a language I could appreciate. That language was direct and powerful and flowed with rhythm and music. Above all, he made the language new. I suppose, being an only child, I could empathise with the alone-ness that pervades his work.

Ever since I took up poetry seriously (my first collection, *Rainsong*, appeared in 1981), I have wanted to translate Ó Ríordáin. Over the years I made several attempts, a number of which appeared in various books of mine with permission from Caoimhín Ó Marcaigh, Ó Ríordáin's publisher, and latterly from Mícheál Ó Conghaile of Cló Iar Chonnacht who now owns the rights to Ó Ríordáin's work. I have decided to put the best of them together with some new translations in a single volume as a homage to Seán Ó Ríordáin. This volume doesn't pretend to be in any way canonical. It contains my favourite Ó Ríordáin poems. They seem to have been among Ó Ríordáin's favourites too – no fewer than nine of them were chosen by him for his 1969 long playing record, *Seán Ó Ríordáin: Filíocht Agus Prós*.

Translating Ó Ríordáin is a challenge – and a pure pleasure. I have tried to translate him sound and sense, keeping as close as I can to his rhythm and rhyme. Others have translated him in free verse, others still in literal prose translations. I leave it to the reader to decide if I have succeeded in bringing Ó Ríordáin over into English. My head is above the parapet. Fire away!

GABRIEL FITZMAURICE

Milking the Sun
Ag Crú na Gréine

Ceol Ceantair

Chuala sé an ceol i gcainteanna Dhún Chaoin,
Ní hiad na focail ach an fonn
A ghabhann trí bhlas is fuaimeanna na Mumhan,
An ceol a chloiseann an strainséir;
Ceol ceantair
Ná cloiseann lucht a labhartha,
Ceol nár chualasa riamh,
Toisc a ghiorracht dom is bhí,
Is mé bheith ar adhastar ag an mbrí.

Ceol a cloistear fós sa Mhumhain,
Fiú in áiteanna 'nar tréigeadh an chanúint.

Local Music

He heard the lilt in the language of Dún Chaoin,
Not the lyrics but the air
That goes through the sounds and flow of Munster,
The music the stranger hears;
A local music
That its speakers do not hear,
A music I never heard
Because I was so near
And I in harness to the sense.

A music you will hear in Munster yet
Even where they've abandoned their dialect.

Siollabadh

Bhí banaltra in otharlann
  I ngile an tráthnóna,
Is cuisleanna i leapachaibh
  Ag preabarnaigh go tomhaiste,
Do sheas sí os gach leaba
  Agus d'fhan sí seal ag comhaireamh
Is do bhreac sí síos an mheadaracht
  Bhí ag siollabadh ina meoraibh,
Is do shiollaib sí go rithimeach
  Fé dheireadh as an seomra,
Is d'fhág 'na diaidh mar chlaisceadal
  Na cuisleanna ag comhaireamh:
Ansin do leath an tAngelus
  Im-shiollabchrith ar bheolaibh,
Ach do tháinig éag ar Amenibh
  Mar chogarnach sa tseomra:
Do leanadh leis an gcantaireacht
  I mainistir na feola,
Na cuisleanna mar mhanachaibh
  Ag siollabadh na nónta.

Syllable-ing

There once was a nurse in a hospital
  In the early part of the evening
And pulses in the patients' beds
  Were beating, beating, beating;
She stood at each bedside
  Taking pulses there awhile
And she noted down their metre
  That beat in rhythmic style
And she syllab-stepped in metre
  Eventually from the ward
Leaving behind a choir of pulses
  As the rhythm flowed:
And then there rang the Angelus
  Syllab-trembling from each bed,
The Amens on the patients' lips
  Were whispered there till dead;
The monastery of the flesh
  Beat out its singing tones,
The pulses like holy monks
  Syllable-ing the nones.

Cúl an Tí

Tá Tír na nÓg ar chúl an tí,
  Tír álainn trína chéile,
Lucht ceithre chos ag siúl na slí
  Gan bróga orthu ná léine,
  Gan Béarla acu ná Gaeilge.

Ach fásann clóca ar gach droim
  Sa tír seo trína chéile,
Is labhartar teanga ar chúl an tí
  Nár thuig aon fhear ach Aesop,
  Is tá sé siúd sa chré anois.

Tá cearca ann is ál sicín,
  Is lacha righin mhothaolach,
Is gadhar mór dubh mar namhaid sa tír
  Ag drannadh le gach éinne,
  Is cat ag crú na gréine.

Sa chúinne thiar tá banc dramhaíl'
  Is iontaisí an tsaoil ann,
Coinnleoir, búclaí, seanhata tuí,
  Is trúmpa balbh néata,
  Is citeal bán mar ghé ann.

Is ann a thagann tincéirí
  Go naofa, trína chéile,
Tá gaol acu le cúl an tí,
  Is bíd ag iarraidh déirce
  Ar chúl gach tí in Éirinn.

Ba mhaith liom bheith ar chúl an tí
  Sa doircheacht go déanach
Go bhfeicinn ann ar chuairt gealaí
  An t-ollaimhín sin Aesop
  Is é ina phúca léannta.

The Back of the House

Translation dedicated to Helena McMahon

At the back of the house is the Land of the Young,
  A higgledy-piggledy place,
Our four footed friends walking all around
  Without shirt or shoe or lace,
  Without a trace of English or Irish.

But on each back there grows a cloak
  In this higgledy-piggledy place,
And a language is spoken at the back of the house
  That no one knows but Aesop
  And he is in the clay now.

Hens are there and chickens too,
  And a duck, the simpleton,
And a big, black dog like an enemy
  Barking at everyone
  And a cat milking the sun.

In the corner there's a heap of junk
  With every kind of wonder,
A candlestick, buckles, an old straw hat,
  A lovely, silent trumpet
  And a white kettle like a goose there.

It's here, too, the travellers come
  Saintly in their disorder,
They are kin to the back of the house
  And they beg for alms there
  At the back of every house in Ireland.

I'd like to be at the back of the house
  In the darkness, late in the evening,
That I could see in the moonlight there
  Little Professor Aesop
  That wise and learned fairy.

Súile Donna

Is léi na súile donna so
A chím i bplaosc a mic,
Ba theangmháil le háilleacht é,
A súile a thuirlingt ort;

Ba theangmháil phribhléideach é,
Lena meabhair is lena corp,
Is mile bliain ba ghearr leat é,
Is iad ag féachaint ort.

Na súile sin gurbh ise iad,
Is ait liom iad aige,
Is náir liom aghaidh a thabhairt uirthi,
Ó tharla sí i bhfear.

Nuair b'ionann iad is ise dhom,
Is beag a shíleas-sa
Go bhfireannódh na súile sin
A labhradh baineann liom.

Cá bhfaighfí údar mearbhaill
Ba mheasa ná é seo?
An gcaithfeam malairt agallaimh
A chleachtadh leo anois?

Ní hí is túisce a bhreathnaigh leo,
Ach an oiread lena mac,
Ná ní hé an duine deireanach
A chaithfidh iad dar liom.

Ab shin a bhfuil de shíoraíocht ann,
Go maireann smut dár mblas,
Trí bhaineannú is fireannú,
Ón máthair go dtí an mac?

Brown Eyes

These brown eyes I see are hers
Now in her son's head,
It was a thing most beautiful
That you inherited;

It was a meeting privileged
With her mind and body too,
For a thousand years would pass so swift
If they but looked at you.

Because those eyes belong to her
It's strange that he has them,
I'm ashamed to face her now because
She happened in a man.

When she and they were one to me
Little did I think
Those eyes would change to masculine
That spoke so womanly.

Where is the source of madness
That's any worse than this?
Do I have to change my dialogue
Now that they are his?

She wasn't the first to see with them
Any more than he
Nor will he be the last
Who will wear them.

Is this all there is of eternity
That something of us lives on
Becoming masculine and feminine
From the mother to the son?

Malairt

"Gaibh i leith," arsa Turnbull, "go bhfeice tú an brón
  I súilibh an chapaill,
Dá mbeadh crúba chomh mór leo sin fútsa bheadh brón
  Id shúilibh chomh maith leis."

Agus b'fhollas gur thuigh sé chomh maith sin an brón
  I súilibh an chapaill,
Is gur mhachnaigh chomh cruaidh air gur tumadh é fá dheoidh
  In aigne an chapaill.

D'fhéachas ar an gcapall go bhfeicinn an brón
  'Na shúilibh ag seasamh,
Do chonac súile Turnbull ag féachaint im threo
  As cloigeann an chapaill.

D'fhéachas ar Turnbull is d'fhéachas air fá dhó
  Is do chonac ar a leacain
Na súile rómhóra bhí balbh le brón —
  Súile an chapaill.

Change

"Come over," said Turnbull, "and look at the sorrow
  In the horse's eyes.
If you had hooves like those under you,
  There would be sorrow in your eyes."

And 'twas plain that he knew the sorrow so well
  In the horse's eyes,
And he wondered so deeply that he dived in the end
  Into the horse's mind.

I looked at the horse then that I might see
  The sorrow in his eyes,
And Turnbull's eyes were looking at me
  From the horse's head.

I looked at Turnbull and looked once again
  And there in Turnbull's head –
Not Turnbull's eyes, but, dumb with grief,
  Were the horse's eyes instead.

An Feairín

Ní Ezra Pound atá i gceist anseo, ach duine de na cainteorií dúchais
Gaeilge is binne agus is oilte sa tír. Ní fear beag é ach an oiread ach
taibhsítear don té a chíonn é go bhfuil gach ball dá bhaill beag toisc
go bhfuil cuma na huaiselachta ar a phearsa.

"Theastódh tigh is gort ón bhfeairín bocht,"
A dúirt an bhean 'dtaobh Pound,
Is bhailigh Pound isteach sa bhfocal di
Is chónaigh ann.

Ní fhaca Pound iomlán go ndúirt sí é,
Is do scrúdaíos é ó bhonn
Fé ghnéithe an teidil sin a bhaist sí air,
Is dar liom gur dheas a rogha.

Tá beirthe ar Phound sa bhfocal sin aici,
Mar feairín is ea Pound,
Do réitigh gach a bhfuil dá chabhail sa bheatha léi,
Ó bharr a chinn go bonn.

Tá buanaíocht age Pound sa bhfocal sin,
Tá suaimhneas aige ann,
Is pé duine eile 'bheidh míshocair inár n'aigne,
Ní mar sin a bheidh Pound.

The Little Man

Ezra Pound is not the man in question here, but one of the sweet-
est and best native Irish speakers in Ireland. Neither is he a small
man but whoever sees him imagines that every part of his body is
small because of his noble appearance.

"He'd need a house and land, the poor *little* man,"
The woman said about Pound
And she gathered him into that word
And he found a home there.

I'd never seen Pound till she pronounced
And I examined him, head to foot,
Under the appearance she bestowed on him
And I thought her choice was good.

Pound is captured in her word
For a little man is Pound,
All he is in this world agrees
From his head down to the ground.

Pound is immortal in that word,
He's contented there
And whoever else in our minds is unsettled,
Pound won't be that way.

Adhlacadh mo Mháthar

Grian an Mheithimh in úllghort,
　Is sioscarnach i síoda an tráthnóna,
Beach mhallaithe ag portaireacht
　Mar screadstracadh ar an nóinbhrat.

Seanlitir shalaithe á léamh agam,
　Le gach focaldeoch dar ólas
Pian bhinibeach ag dealgadh mo chléibhse,
　Do bhrúigh amach gach focal díobh a dheoir féin.

Do chuimhníos ar an láimh a dhein an scríbhinn,
　Lámh a bhí inaitheanta mar aghaidh,
Lámh a thál riamh cneastacht seana-Bhíobla,
　Lámh a bhí mar bhalsam is tú tinn.

Agus thit an Meitheamh siar isteach sa Gheimhreadh,
　Den úllghort deineadh reilig bhán cois abhann,
Is i lár na balbh-bháine i mo thimpeall
　Do lúigh os ard sa tsneachta an dúpholl,

Gile gearrachaile lá a céad chomaoine,
　Gile abhlainne Dé Domhnaigh ar altóir,
Gile bainne ag sreangtheitheadh as na cíochaibh,
　Nuair a chuireadar mo mháthair, gile an fhóid.

Bhí m'aigne á sciúirseadh féin ag iarraidh
　An t-adhlacadh a bhlaiseadh go hiomlán,
Nuair a d'eitil tríd an gciúnas bán go míonla
　Spideog a bhí gan mhearbhall gan scáth:

Agus d'fhan os cionn na huaighe fé mar go mb'eol di
　Go raibh an toisc a thug í ceilte ar chách
Ach an té a bhí ag feitheamh ins an gcomhrainn,
　Is do rinneas éad fén gcaidreamh neamhghnách.

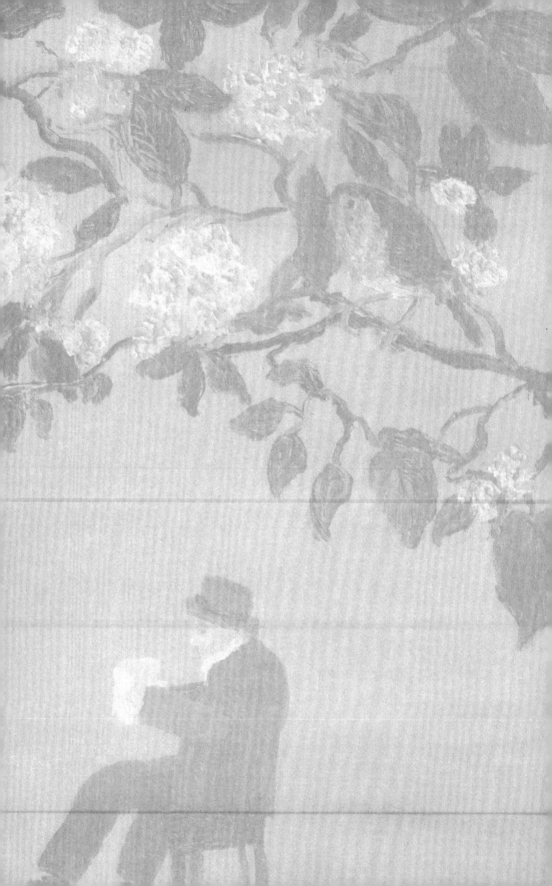

Do thuirling aer na bhFlaitheas ar an uaigh sin,
   Bhí meidhir uafásach naofa ar an éan,
Bhíos deighilte amach ón diamhairghnó im thuata,
   Is an uaigh sin os mo chomhair in imigéin.

Le cumhracht bróin do folcadh m'anam drúiseach,
   Thit sneachta geanmnaíochta ar mo chroí,
Anois adhlacfad sa chroí a deineadh ionraic
   Cuimhne na mná d'iompair mé trí ráithe ina broinn.

Tháinig na scológa le borbthorann sluasad,
   Is do scuabadar le fuinneamh an chré isteach san uaigh,
D'fhéachas-sa treo eile, bhí comharsa ag glanadh a ghlúine,
   D'fhéachas ar an sagart is bhí saoltacht ina ghnúis.

Grian an Mheithimh in úllghort,
   Is sioscarnach i síoda an tráthnóna,
Beach mhallaithe ag portaireacht
   Mar screadstracadh ar an nóinbhrat.

Ranna beaga bacacha á scríobh agam,
   Ba mhaith liom breith ar eireaball spideoige,
Ba mhaith liom sprid lucht glanta glún a dhíbirt,
   Ma mhaith liom triall go deireadh lae go brónach.

My Mother's Burial

June sun in the orchard
  And a silken rustling in the fading day,
An infernal bee humming
  Like a screamtearing of the evening's veil.

I was reading an old, soiled letter,
  And every word-drink I imbibed
Thorned my heart with bitter pain;
  At every single word I read, I cried.

I remembered then the hand that wrote the letter,
  A hand recognisable as a face,
A hand that bestowed the mildness of an old Bible,
  A hand that was like balsam to my pain.

And then the June fell over into winter
  And the orchard became a white cemetery by a stream,
And amid the silent whiteness all around me
  Through the snow I could hear the black hole scream.

The brightness of a girl on the day of her First Communion,
  The brightness of the host on Sunday on the altar of God,
The brightness of milk flowing freely from the breasts,
  When they buried my mother, the brightness of the sod.

While my mind was scourging itself with trying
  To taste my mother's burial, whole, complete,
Through the white silence flew so gently
  A robin, unflustered, without fear.

She remained above the grave as if knowing
  That the reason for her coming was concealed
To all but the one lying waiting in the coffin
  And I was jealous of this strange intimacy.

The air of Heaven descended on that grave there,
  There was a terrible, holy mirth about that robin,
I was cut off from the mystery like a layman,
  The grave was far away though I was beside the coffin.

My lustful soul was cleansed with sweetest sorrow,
  On my heart there fell a snow of purity,
In the heart that was made upright I will bury
  The memory of her who carried me for three seasons.

The strong men began with their rude shovels
  And roughly swept the earth into her grave;
I looked the other way, a neighbour was brushing his knees clean,
  I looked at the priest and saw worldliness in his face.

June sun in the orchard
  And a silken rustling in the fading day,
An infernal bee humming
  Like a screamtearing of the evening's veil.

I am writing small, uneven verses,
  I would like to catch a robin's tail,
I would like to banish the knee-brushing spirit,
  To journey sadly to the end of day.

Reo

Maidin sheaca ghabhas amach
Is bhí seál póca romham ar sceach,
Rugas air le cur im phóca
Ach sciorr sé uaim mar bhí sé reoite:
Ní héadach beo a léim óm ghlaic
Ach rud fuair bás aréir ar sceach:
Is siúd ag taighde mé fé m'intinn
Go bhfuaireas macasamhail an ní seo —
   Lá dar phógas bean dem mhuintir
   Is í ina cónra reoite, sínte.

Freeze

One morning I went out in the frost,
There was a handkerchief before me on a bush,
To put it in my pocket, I took hold
But it slipped from me because it was frozen:
No living cloth slipped from my grasp
But a thing that died last night on a bush:
I searched my mind until I could bring
To it a likeness for this thing —
　The day I kissed a woman of my kin
　And she in her coffin, laid out, frozen.

Oíche Nollaig na mBan

Bhí fuinneamh sa stoirm a éalaigh aréir,
   Aréir Oíche Nollaig na mBan,
As gealt-teach iargúlta tá laistiar den ré
   Is do scréach tríd an spéir chughainn 'na gealt,
Gur ghíosc geataí comharsan mar ghogallach gé,
   Gur bhúir abhainn shlaghdánach mar tharbh,
Gur múcadh mo choinneal mar bhuille ar mo bhéal
   A las 'na splanc obann an fhearg.

Ba mhaith liom go dtiocfadh an stoirm sin féin
   An oíche go mbeadsa go lag
Ag filleadh abhaile ó rince an tsaoil
   Is solas an pheaca ag dul as,
Go líonfaí gach neomat le liúrigh ón spéir,
   Go ndéanfaí den domhan scuaine scread,
Is ná cloisfinn an ciúnas ag gluaiseacht fám dhéin,
   Ná inneall an ghluaisteáin ag stad.

The Women's Christmas Eve

The storm escaped with a fury last night
  (Last night was the Women's Christmas Eve)
From the desolate bedlam that's concealed by the moon
  Through the sky, like a madman it screeched
Till my neighbours' gates grated like gaggling geese,
  Till the river's wheeze bellowed, a bull,
Till my candle was quenched like a blow to my mouth
  That reddened my anger in full.

I'd like that a storm would blow up like that
  The night that I'm weakening, and fail
Going back home from the great dance of life
  With the light of sin on the wane;
That each moment be filled with shouts from the sky,
  That the world be one screaming mass
So I won't hear the silence approaching my way
  Or the engine of the car as it stops.

An Bás

Bhí an bás lem ais,
D'aontaíos dul
Gan mhoill gan ghol,
Bhíos am fhéinmheas
Le hionadh:
A dúrtsa
"Agus b'shin mise
Go hiomlán,
Mhuise slán
Leat, a dhuine."

Ag féachaint siar dom anois
Ar an dtráth
Go dtáinig an bás
Chugham fé dheithneas,
Is go mb'éigean
Domsa géilleadh,
Measaim go dtuigim
Lúcháir béithe
Ag siúl le chéile,
Cé ná fuilim baineann.

Death

Death was beside me,
I agreed to go
Without delay or woe,
I was examining my life
With wonder:
I said
'And that was I
In total,
Well, goodbye,
My boy'.

Looking back now
On the time
When death came to me
Hurriedly
And I had to yield,
I think I understand
The joy of a maiden
As she waits for her lover
Though I am no woman.

Claustrophobia

In aice an fhíona
Tá coinneal is sceon,
Tá dealbh mo Thiarna
D'réir dealraimh gan chomhacht,
Tá a dtiocfaidh den oíche
Mar shluaite sa chlós,
Tá rialtas na hoíche
Lasmuigh den bhfuinneoig;
Má mhúchann mo choinneal
Ar ball de m'ainneoin
Léimfidh an oíche
Isteach im scámhóig,
Sárófar m'intinn
Is ceapfar dom sceon,
Déanfar díom oíche,
Bead im dhoircheacht bheo:
    Ach má mhaireann mo choinneal
    Aon oíche amháin
    Bead im phoblacht solais
    Gu dtiocfaidh an lá

Claustrophobia

Beside the wine
A candle, fear,
The statue of my Lord
Has no power here,
What will come of the night
Is crowding outside,
Beyond my window
Are the powers of the night;
If my candle should quench
In spite of me soon,
The night will jump
Straight into my lung,
My mind, overcome,
Will be turned into fright,
A living darkness,
I'll be turned into night:
    But if my candle survives
    This one night
    Until day comes
    I'll be a republic of light.

Oileán agus Oileán Eile

I: Roimh Dhul ar Oileán Bharra Naofa

Tá Sasanach ag iascaireacht sa loch,
Tá an fhírinne rólom ar an oileán,
Ach raghad i measc na gcuimhne agus na gcloch,
Is nífead le mórurraim mo dhá láimh.

Raghad anonn is éistfead san oileán,
Éistfead seal le smaointe smeara naomh
A thiomnaigh Barra Naofa don oileán,
Éistfead leo in inchinn an aeir.

II: Amhras iar nDul ar an Oileán

A Bharra, is aoibhinn liom aoibhneas do thí
Agus caraimse áitreabh do smaointe,
Ach ní feas dom an uaitse na smaointe airím
Mar tá daoscar ar iostas im intinn.

Le bréithre gan bhrí,
Le bodhaire na mblian,
Thuirling clúmh liath
Ar mo smaointe.

Mar chloich a cúnlaíodh
Do hadhlacadh iad,
Do truailleadh a gclaíomh
Im intinn.

Naoimh is leanaí
A bhogann clúmh liath
De cheannaithe Chríost
Nó do smaointe.

Tá an t-aer mar mheánfuíoch
Ar m'anam 'na luí,
Bhfuil Barra sa ghaoith
Am líonadh?

Tá Barra is na naoimh
Na cianta sa chria
Is dalladh púicín
Ad bhíogadh.

Tá tuirse im chroí
Den bhfocal gan draíocht,
Bíodh dalladh no diabhal
Am shiabhradh.

III: An Bíogadh

Tá ráflaí naomh san aer máguaird
Is an ghaoth ag fuáil tríd,
Tá paidir sheanda im chuimhne i léig,
Is mo smaointe á séideadh arís.

Anseo ar bhuaile smaointe naomh
Do léim chugham samhail nua,
Do chuala tarcaisne don saol
I nguth an éin bhí 'clagar ceoil.

An ceol a raid sé leis an mbith
Dob shin oileán an éin,
Níl éinne beo nach bhfuair oileán,
Is trua a chás má thréig.

IV: Oileán Gach Éinne

I bhfírinne na haigne
Tá oileán séin,
Is tusa tá ar mharthain ann
Is triall fád dhéin,
Ná bíodh ort aon chritheagla
Id láthair féin,
Cé go loiscfidh sé id bheatha tú,
Do thusa féin,
Mar níl ionat ach eascaine
A dúirt an saol,
Níl ionat ach cabaireacht
Ó bhéal go béal:
Cé gur cumadh tú id phaidir gheal
Ar bhéal mhic Dé
Do scoiltis-se do thusa ceart
Le dúil sa tsaol,
Ach is paidir fós an tusa sin
Ar oileán séin,
A fhan go ciúin ag cogarnach
Ar bheolaibh Dé
Nuair do rincis-se go macnasach
Ar ghob an tsaoil.

V: Oileán Bharra Naofa

Tráthnóna ceathach sa Ghuagán,
Ceo ag creimeadh faille,
Do chuardaíos comhartha ar oileán,
Do fuaireas é i gcrannaibh.

Im thimpeall d'eascair crainn chasfháis,
Dob achrannach a leagan
Do lúbadar 'ngach uile aird
Mar chorp á dhó ina bheatha.

Mar scríbhinn breacaithe ar phár
Is scríbhinn eile trasna air
Chonac geanc is glún is cruit is spág,
Fá dheoidh chonac dealramh Gandhi.

A Bharra, chím i lúib na ngéag
Gur troideadh comhrac aonair
Idir thusa Dé is tusa an tsaoil
Anseo id gheanclainn naofa.

Nuair ghlanann ceo na feola léi
Tig áilleacht ait i rocaibh,
Is féidir cló a mheas ann féin
Sa tsolas cnámhach folamh.

Tá sult na saoirse i gcló na gcrann
Is grá don tsúil a fiaradh,
Tá dúil sa rud tá casta cam
Is gráin don bhog is don díreach.

Is fireann scríbhinn seo na gcrann,
Níl cíoch ná cuar in aon bhall,
Tá manach scríte abhus is thall,
Sé Barra lúb na ngéag seo.

A insint féin ar Fhlaitheas Dé,
Ag sin oileán gach éinne,
Ag Críost atá ina fhuil ag scéith
An casadh tá ina bhréithre.

Is macasamhail dá oileán féin
Oileán seo Bharra Naofa,
An Críost a bhí ina fhuil ag scéith
An phúcaíocht ait i ngéagaibh.

VI: An Sasanach agus Mé Féin

Tá Sasanach ag iascaireacht sa loch
Is measaimse gur beag leis an t-oileán,
Ach ní feasach dom nach iascaireacht ar loch
Don Sasanach bheith ionraic ar oileán.

Raghad anonn is fágfad an t-oileán,
Fágfad slán le smaointe smeara naomh,
Raghad ag ceilt na fírinne mar chách,
Raghad anonn ag cabaireacht sa tsaol.

An Island and Another Island

Translation dedicated to Theo Dorgan

I: Before Going on Saint Barra's Island

An Englishman is fishing in the lake,
On Barra's island the naked truth is found,
I'll wash my hands with great respect
Among the memories and the stony ground.

I'll go and listen on the island,
I'll listen to the essential thoughts of saints
That holy Barra bequeathed to the island,
I'll listen to them in the brain of the air.

II: Doubt after Going on the Island

Barra, sweet to me is the sweetness of your home
And I love the place wherein your thoughts I find
But I don't know if the thoughts I feel are yours
Because a rot is lodging in my mind.

With meaningless words,
With the deafness of the years
A grey down descended
On my thoughts here.

Like a stone in a narrow space
They were buried, confined,
Their sword sharpness was dulled
In my mind.

Only children and saints
Dispel the grey down
From Christ's face
Or from thoughts.

The air is yawning
On my sleeping spirit,
Is Barra in the wind
Filling it?

Barra and his saints
Are long in their graves
And confusion like a blindfold
Is waking in you.

My heart is weary
Of the magicless word,
Whether from blindfold or devil
In delusion I'm stirred.

III: The Quickening

The stories of saints are in the air all around
And the wind threads through them here,
My thoughts are blowing strong again
In an old half-forgotten prayer.

Here in this place of saintly thoughts,
A new image came to me
In the voice of a bird that flung out
Contempt for the life we lead.

The music that he flung at the world,
That was his own island,
There's no one alive that hasn't one
And woe to him who's abandoned it.

IV: Each One's Island

In the truth of the mind,
There's an island there
And you who live in that place
Must dare to seek yourself,
Don't be afraid
In your own presence where
Your self would destroy you
In its fire,
For you're only a curse
The world swears,
You're only a babbling
Going from mouth to mouth there.
Though on Christ's mouth
You were formed a prayer,
You've split yourself
With worldly desire,
But on this island
You remain a prayer,
Still quietly whispered
On God's lips there
While you danced on the world's beak
Playfully.

V: Saint Barra's Island

A rainy evening in Gougane Barra,
Fog gnawing at the cliffs,
I sought a sign there on the island
And I found it in the trees.

Around me sprang up trees all twisted,
In every direction they twisted and turned
So distorted they appeared there
Like a body being burned.

Like a script upon a parchment
And across it another hand,
I saw a nose, a knee, a hump, a clumsy foot,
And, in the end, the image of Gandhi.

Barra, I see in the twisted branches
That you fought your battle alone
Between your God-self and your worldly self
Here in your saintly home.

When the mist of flesh-and-blood disperses,
There's a strange beauty in furrowed things, I find,
One can measure truth there
In the empty, skeletal light.

There's the joy of freedom in the shapes of the trees
And love for the eye they changed,
There's love for the crooked, twisted thing
And disdain for the soft and straight.

The tree-script here is masculine,
Neither breast nor curve appears,
Monk is written all around,
Barra is these bending trees.

The island tells his own story
Of God's heaven, each to each,
The Christ that in his blood is flowing
Shapes his speech.

Barra's island is an image
Of each one's island, each one's soul,
The Christ that in our blood is flowing
Is in the haunted branches we behold.

VI: The Englishman and Myself

An Englishman is fishing in the lake,
And of these things he's probably unaware,
Maybe he's found the integrity of his own island
Fishing in the lake.

I'll go and leave the island,
The thoughts of saints I'll leave behind,
I'll go and hide the truth like everyone else
In idle speech throughout my life.

GABRIEL FITZMAURICE was born, in 1952, in the village of Moyvane, Co. Kerry where he still lives. For over thirty years he taught in the local primary school from which he retired as principal in 2007. He is author of more than fifty books, including collections of poetry in English and Irish as well as several collections of verse for children. He has translated extensively from the Irish and has edited a number of anthologies of poetry in English and Irish. He has published two volumes of essays and collections of songs and ballads. Poems of his have been set to music and recorded by Brian Kennedy and performed by the RTÉ Cór na nÓg with the RTÉ National Symphony Orchestra. He frequently broadcasts on radio and television on culture and the arts.

He has been described as "the best contemporary, traditional, popular poet in English" in Booklist (U.S), "a wonderful poet" in the Guardian, "one of Ireland's leading poets" and "poetry's answer to John B. Keane" in Books Ireland, "Ireland's favourite poet for children" in Best Books! and "the Irish A.A. Milne" by Declan Kiberd in the Sunday Tribune.

BOOKS BY GABRIEL FITZMAURICE

POETRY IN ENGLISH

Rainsong (Beaver Row Press, Dublin, 1984)

Road to the Horizon (Beaver Row Press, 1987)

Dancing Through (Beaver Row Press, 1990)

The Father's Part (Story Line Press, Oregon, 1992)

The Space Between: New and Selected Poems 1984-1992
(Cló Iar-Chonnachta, Conamara, 1993)

The Village Sings (Story Line Press; Cló Iar-Chonnachta;
Peterloo Poets, Cornwall, 1996)

A Wrenboy's Carnival: Poems 1980-2000
(Wolfhound Press, Dublin, Peterloo Poets, 2000)

I and the Village (Marino Books, Dublin, 2002)

The Boghole Boys (Marino Books, Cork, 2005)

Twenty-One Sonnets (Salmon Poetry, Cliffs of Moher, 2007)

The Essential Gabriel Fitzmaurice (Mercier Press, Cork 2008)

In Praise of Football (Mercier Press, 2009)

Poems of Faith and Doubt (Salmon Poetry, 2011)

A Middle-aged Orpheus Looks Back at his Life (Liberties Press, Dublin, 2013)

The Lonesome Road: Collected and New Poems 1984-2014 (Liberties Press, 2014)

POETRY IN IRISH

Nocht (Coiscéim, Dublin, 1989)

Ag Síobshiúl Chun An Rince (Coiscéim, 1995)

Giolla na nAmhrán: Dánta 1988 1998 (Coiscéim, 1998)

CHILDREN'S POETRY IN ENGLISH

The Moving Stair (The Kerryman, Tralee, 1989)

The Moving Stair (Enlarged edition – Poolbeg Press, Dublin, 1993)

But Dad! (Poolbeg Press, 1995)

Puppy and the Sausage (Poolbeg Press, 1998)

Dear Grandad (Poolbeg Press, 2001)

A Giant Never Dies (Poolbeg Press, 2002)

The Oopsy Kid (Poolbeg Press, 2003)

Don't Squash Fluffy (Poolbeg Press, 2004)

I'm Proud to be Me (Mercier Press, 2005)

Really Rotten Rhymes (Mercier Press, 2007)

GF Woz Ere (Mercier Press, 2009)

Splat (Mercier Press, 2012)

Will you be my Friend? (Liberties Press, 2016)

Will you be my Friend? (Revised edition –Salmon Poetry, 2017)

CHILDREN'S POETRY IN IRISH
Nach Iontach Mar Atá (Cló Iar-Chonnachta, 1994)

CHILDREN'S POETRY IN ENGLISH AND IRISH
Do Teachers Go to the Toilet? / An dTéann Múinteoirí go Tigh an Asail? (Mercier Press, 2010)

ESSAYS
Kerry on my Mind (Salmon Publishing, Cliffs of Moher, 1999)
Beat the Goatskin Till the Goat Cries (Mercier Press, 2006)

TRANSLATION
The Purge (A translation of *An Phurgóid* by Mícheál Ó hAirtnéide) (Beaver Row Press, 1989)
Poems I Wish I'd Written: Translations from the Irish (Cló Iar-Chonnachta, 1996)
The Rhino's Specs / Spéaclaí an tSrónbheannaigh: Selected Children's Poems of Gabriel Rosenstock
    (Mercier Press, 2002)
Poems from the Irish: Collected Translations (Marino Books, 2004)
Ventry Calling (Mercier Press, 2005)
House, Don't Fall on Me (Mercier Press, 2007)
Lucinda Sly: A Woman Hanged (Liberties Press, 2013)
An Island Community: The Ebb and Flow of the Great Blasket Island (Liberties Press, 2015)

EDITOR
The Flowering Tree / An Crann Faoi Bhláth (contemporary poetry in Irish
with verse translations) with Declan Kiberd (Wolfhound Press, 1991)
Between the Hills and Sea: Songs and Ballads of Kerry (Oidhreacht, Ballyheigue, 1991)
Con Greaney: Traditional Singer (Oidhreacht, 1991)
Homecoming / An Bealach 'na Bhaile: Selected Poems of Cathal Ó Searcaigh (Cló Iar-Chonnachta, 1993)
Irish Poetry Now: Other Voices (Wolfhound Press, 1993)
Kerry Through Its Writers (New Island Books, Dublin, 1993)
The Listowel Literary Phenomenon: North Kerry Writers – A Critical Introduction (Cló Iar-Chonnachta, 1994)
Rusty Nails and Astronauts: A Wolfhound Poetry Anthology (Wolfhound Press, 1999) with Robert Dunbar
'The Boro' and 'The Cross': The Parish of Moyvane-Knockanure (The Moyvane-Knockanure Millennium Book
    Committee, 2000) with Áine Cronin and John Looney
The Kerry Anthology (Marino Books, 2000)
'Come All Good Men and True': Essays from the John B. Keane Symposium (Mercier Press, 2004)
The World of Bryan MacMahon (Mercier Press, 2005)
Best Loved Poems: Favourite Poems from the South of Ireland (Currach Press, Dublin, 2016)

www.salmonpoetry.com

"Like the sea-run Steelhead salmon that thrashes upstream to its spawning ground,
then instead of dying, returns to the sea — Salmon Poetry Press
brings precious cargo to both Ireland and America in the poetry it publishes,
then carries that select work to its readership against incalculable odds."

TESS GALLAGHER